NATURAL DISASTER ZONE

WILDFIRES AND FREAK WEATHER

BEN HUBBARD

D1336066

Franklin Watts
First published in Great Britain in 2019 by The Watts Publishing Group

Credits
Editor: Elise Short
Illustration and Design: Collaborate Agency

Picture credits:
Shutterstock: Eky Studio: cover, 1; seksan wangkeeree : cover, 1;
Chirokung : 9; Dan Ross: 29; 24Novembers: 30.

HB ISBN 978 1 4451 6592 9
PB ISBN 978 1 4451 6593 6

Printed in Dubai

Franklin Watts
An imprint of
Hachette Children's Group
Part of The Watts Publishing Group
Carmelite House
50 Victoria Embankment
London EC4Y 0DZ

An Hachette UK Company
www.hachette.co.uk

www.franklinwatts.co.uk

CONTENTS

Introducing Wildfires and Freak Weather

Freak weather and wildfires are fearsome events which can cause great harm to human life. They are unpredictable, uncontrollable and often catch people unawares. However, these natural disasters inflict very different types of destruction on the world around them. Let's take a closer look at what they are.

What are Wildfires and Freak Weather Events?

Wildfires are ferocious, unplanned fires that burn intensely through natural areas such as forest and grassland.

Freak weather is extreme and unusual weather events, such as flash floods, ice storms, dust storms, heatwaves and drought.

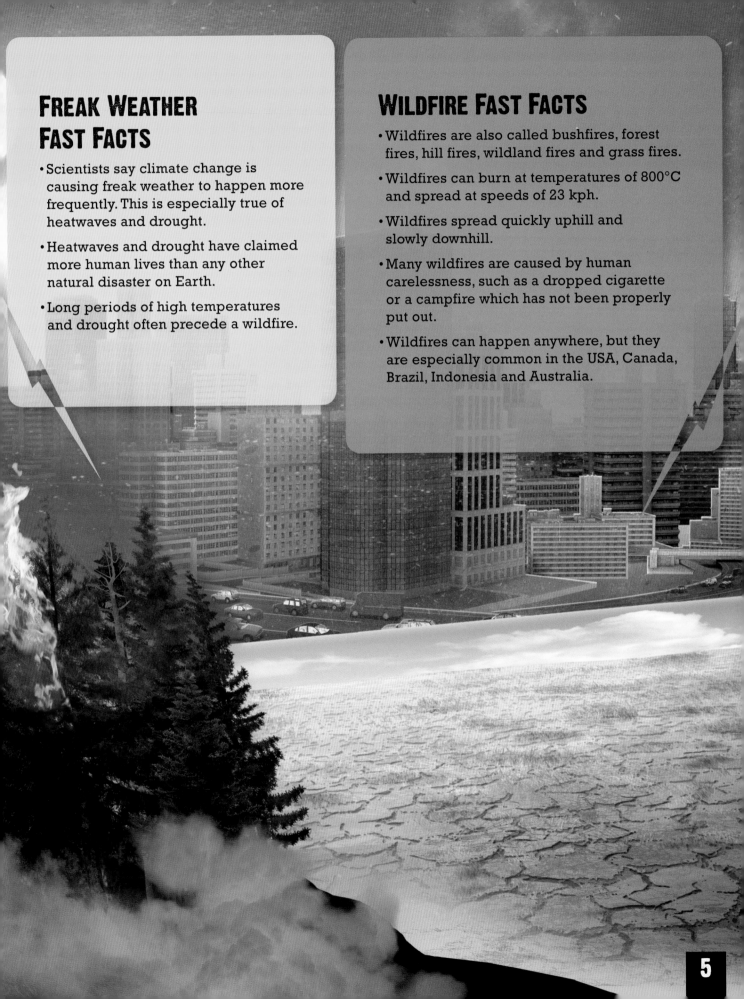

Freak Weather Fast Facts

- Scientists say climate change is causing freak weather to happen more frequently. This is especially true of heatwaves and drought.

- Heatwaves and drought have claimed more human lives than any other natural disaster on Earth.

- Long periods of high temperatures and drought often precede a wildfire.

Wildfire Fast Facts

- Wildfires are also called bushfires, forest fires, hill fires, wildland fires and grass fires.

- Wildfires can burn at temperatures of 800°C and spread at speeds of 23 kph.

- Wildfires spread quickly uphill and slowly downhill.

- Many wildfires are caused by human carelessness, such as a dropped cigarette or a campfire which has not been properly put out.

- Wildfires can happen anywhere, but they are especially common in the USA, Canada, Brazil, Indonesia and Australia.

WHEN A WILDFIRE IGNITES

In June and October 2017, Portugal was struck by the worst wildfires in its history. The wildfires broke out during an intense summer heatwave, when temperatures reached over 40°C. Some of the fires were caused by lightning strikes, but arson was also suspected. Dozens of people were killed in the fires and hundreds of thousands of hectares of land burned.

THE JUNE FIRES

On 17 June, four wildfires struck the Pedrogao Grande area in central Portugal.

Several hundred firefighters and 160 fire engines were sent to battle the blaze. But by that evening, 60 more fires had erupted around the country. Many people were caught by the flames and perished in their cars as they tried to escape. After five days the fires were brought under control, but 64 people had died.

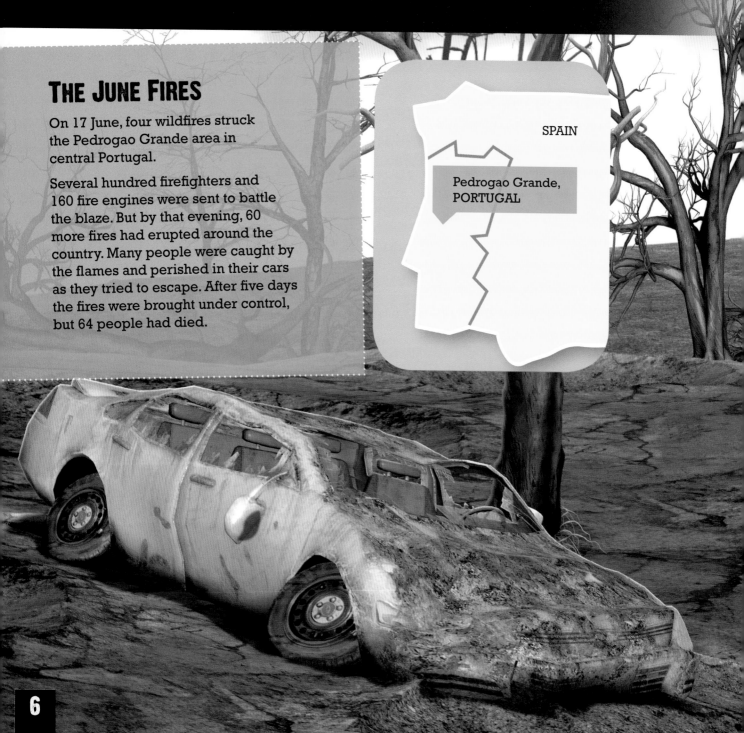

SPAIN

Pedrogao Grande, PORTUGAL

THE OCTOBER FIRES

On 13 October, hundreds of wildfires once again erupted across northern Portugal, and north-western Spain, fanned by winds from nearby Hurricane Ophelia.

For five days, over 4,000 firefighters fought the flames, aided by pilots dumping water from planes. After the flames were brought under control, the death toll had reached 45 in Portugal and four in Spain.

FASTER DISASTER FACTS

• The large number of fast-burning pine and eucalyptus trees contributed to the quick spread of the June wildfires.

• Over 520,000 hectares of Portuguese land was burned during both the June and October wildfires.

• A mixture of smoke from the October wildfires and Saharan sand blown into the atmosphere brought a strange orange colour to European skies.

• Soot from the October wildfires caused black rain to fall on Estonia.

ARSONISTS AND CLIMATE CHANGE

On the worst day of the October wildfires, firefighters were battling over 400 fires at the same time. Although officials found that some of the June fires had been caused by lightning, over 61 suspected arsonists were also arrested on suspicion of starting some of the fires.

Portugal is a warm country vulnerable to wildfires. However, experts say climate change has lengthened the wildfire season from two to five months. This is predicted to have an ongoing impact on the frequency of Portuguese wildfires in the future.

TYPES OF WILDFIRE

Every wildfire begins with a single spark. This can be caused by a lightning strike, a volcanic eruption or even the heat from the Sun. Wildfires are also started by people. Cigarettes thrown from cars and out-of-control campfires are common causes. Some people, called arsonists, start wildfires deliberately.

WILDFIRE TYPES

Wildfires fall into three main types. The way a fire burns, or behaves, determines what type of wildfire it is. The three types are: ground fire, surface fire and crown fire. Sometimes all three types can occur within the same wildfire.

SURFACE FIRE

A surface fire moves across the forest floor, burning leaves, fallen branches and plant litter. Surface fires often move fast and do little damage to trees. Certain trees, such as Douglas firs, have adapted to cope with surface fires. Their bark is thicker and their branches grow higher up. Ecosystems usually recover quickly from surface fires.

GROUND FIRE

A ground fire is a slow-moving fire that burns beneath rotting wood and decomposing leaves that cover the forest floor. Because they usually burn underground, ground fires are dangerous, hard to detect and difficult to put out. They are a disaster for ecosystems as they can smolder away under a layer of snow all winter, before flaring up again in the spring.

CROWN FIRE

A crown fire burns in the 'crown', or treetops. Crown fires are intense, dangerous wildfires that spread quickly. Entire forests can burn down during a large crown fire. They are hard to put out because the wind can cause them to change direction suddenly. Crown fires often cause great destruction to people and property.

WEATHER AND WILDFIRES

Wildfires occur most commonly in countries with hot, dry weather. Heatwaves, drought and strong winds all contribute to a wildfire's ferocity. In Australia, a dry wind caused by a climate cycle called El Niño often fans the flames of its bushfires.

PARTS OF A WILDFIRE

To start, survive and spread, a wildfire needs heat, fuel and oxygen. Once it has all three elements, a wildfire begins to burn and spread outwards. It usually moves in the direction of the wind.

ANATOMY OF A WILDFIRE

As it spreads, a wildfire takes on a recognisable pattern, which is made up of several particular parts. These parts are shown below.

The **flanks** are the side parts of the wildfire's perimeter, or edge.

The **point of origin** is where the wildfire starts. From there, it spreads outwards.

The **heel** is the part of the wildfire directly opposite the head (see page 11). This is the slowest-spreading part of the fire.

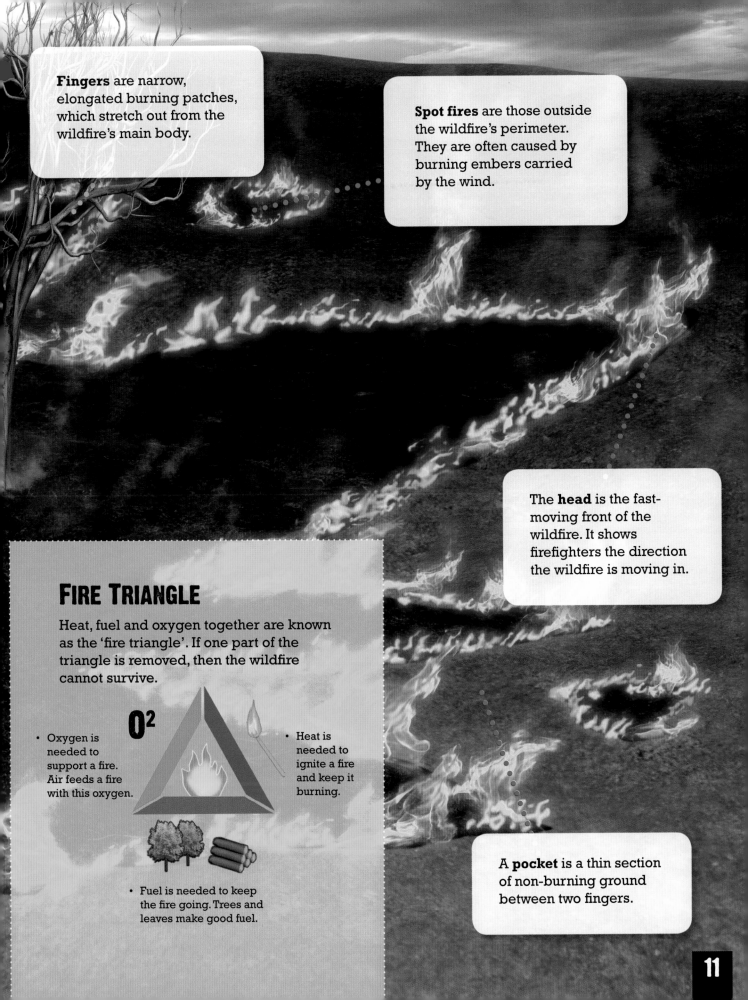

Fingers are narrow, elongated burning patches, which stretch out from the wildfire's main body.

Spot fires are those outside the wildfire's perimeter. They are often caused by burning embers carried by the wind.

The **head** is the fast-moving front of the wildfire. It shows firefighters the direction the wildfire is moving in.

FIRE TRIANGLE

Heat, fuel and oxygen together are known as the 'fire triangle'. If one part of the triangle is removed, then the wildfire cannot survive.

O^2

- Oxygen is needed to support a fire. Air feeds a fire with this oxygen.

- Heat is needed to ignite a fire and keep it burning.

- Fuel is needed to keep the fire going. Trees and leaves make good fuel.

A **pocket** is a thin section of non-burning ground between two fingers.

CASE STUDY: VICTORIA, 2009

On 7 February 2009, the Australian state of Victoria was struck by a series of deadly bushfires. The fires quickly became the most devastating in the country's history. They would result in 173 fatalities, 414 injuries, the loss of over one million animals and more than 450,000 hectares of land burned.

Victoria, AUSTRALIA

BUSHFIRE BUILD-UP

In February 2009, Victoria was in the grip of a two-month-long heatwave. In the city of Melbourne, temperatures reached 45°C and conditions in the bush became tinder-dry. Then, on Saturday, 7 February, hot winds reaching 100 kph brought down power lines in the district of Kilmore East. A spark from the power lines then set a fire alight.

THE HUMAN COST

Although many small fires raged, one large wildfire struck the town of Kinglake. Here, 330,000 hectares were burned, 1,800 houses were destroyed and 159 were lives lost.

Altogether, the fires destroyed over 3,500 buildings, including 2,029 homes. In addition, 7,562 people were displaced by the disaster, which became known as the Black Saturday bushfires.

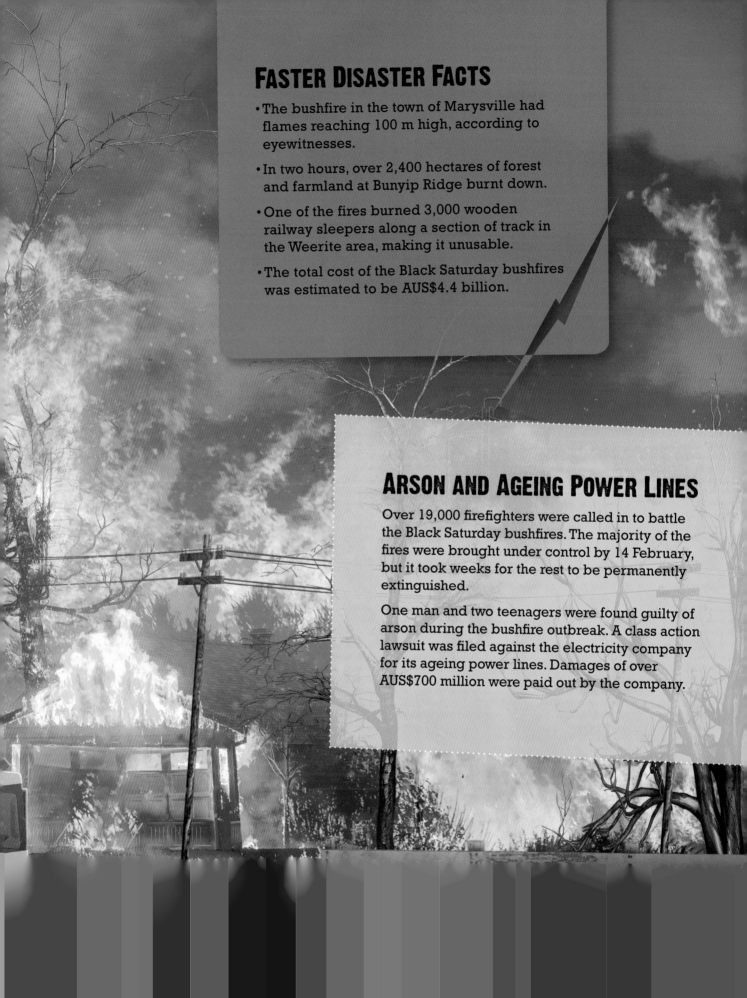

Faster Disaster Facts

- The bushfire in the town of Marysville had flames reaching 100 m high, according to eyewitnesses.

- In two hours, over 2,400 hectares of forest and farmland at Bunyip Ridge burnt down.

- One of the fires burned 3,000 wooden railway sleepers along a section of track in the Weerite area, making it unusable.

- The total cost of the Black Saturday bushfires was estimated to be AUS$4.4 billion.

Arson and Ageing Power Lines

Over 19,000 firefighters were called in to battle the Black Saturday bushfires. The majority of the fires were brought under control by 14 February, but it took weeks for the rest to be permanently extinguished.

One man and two teenagers were found guilty of arson during the bushfire outbreak. A class action lawsuit was filed against the electricity company for its ageing power lines. Damages of over AUS$700 million were paid out by the company.

WILDFIRE FIGHTERS

Wildfire firefighters use a number of special strategies to get a fire under control. They also employ different experts for different sections of the fire.

ENGINE CREWS

Engine crews are the fearless, front-line wildfire fighters who are often first to tackle the flames. They us fire engines and hoses to douse the wildfire.

WILDLAND FIREFIGHTERS

Wildland firefighters are the crews that dig out ditches of soil, rock and tree stumps to create a firebreak that a wildfire can't cross. A wildland firefighter's main tool is a pulaski. This is a type of axe with a hoe on the other side for digging and scraping.

HOTSHOT CREWS

The best wildland firefighters can become elite firefighters known as hotshot crews. These experts travel to the wildfire's dangerous 'head' to predict where it will go. They then use chainsaws, explosives and digging equipment to create elaborate firebreaks, wide areas of bare ground to stop the fire's advance.

SMOKEJUMPERS

Smokejumpers are daredevil firefighters who parachute from planes into the middle of a wildfire. Once on the ground, they dig firebreaks to prevent the wildfire spreading. This is an important way of attacking wildfires which occur in remote areas that cannot be reached by fire engines.

HELITACK CREWS

Aeroplanes are often used to drop massive loads of water and fire-retardant liquid on wildfires. 'Helitack' crews also do this from helicopters. Because they can hover and land in awkward areas, helicopters are also used to drop equipment down to smokejumpers on the ground.

PREVENTING FIRE

Scientists study wildfires to better understand how they behave. Their research helps people prevent wildfires and find better ways of tackling them. It also shows us how a wildfire can affect the plants and animals living in a particular area.

SIMULATING WILDFIRES

Scientists working in fire science laboratories create their own fires in wind tunnels to study them. Dry fuel found in forests is fed to these fires to see how it burns. Different levels of oxygen and wind are then pumped into the tunnels to see how the fires react. Finally, fire-retardant liquids are trialled to douse the flames. The results help firefighters adapt their equipment and techniques to battle wildfires in the open.

HELPFUL FIRES

Wildfires are deadly for humans and animals, but they also help new forest life to grow. This is because a fire breaks down plant matter and releases nitrogen into the soil. Nitrogen is an essential nutrient that plants release when they decompose. After a wildfire, this nutrient-rich soil and the higher levels of sunlight, due to the absence of tall trees, create good growing conditions. Quickly, new plants spring to life and the forest is renewed. Some trees have seeds that are triggered by fire as well.

CLIMATE CHANGE

Scientists say that more frequent heatwaves and drought caused by climate change are increasing wildfire activity. Experts believe increased funding into wildfire research and prevention is the only way to combat large loss of life in the future.

WILDFIRES AROUND THE WORLD

Scientists study wildfires around the world from satellite images. In the map above, the pink areas are a record of a wildfire. Brazil, Indonesia, Canada, Australia and the United States are all vast countries that experience at least one large wildfire every year. In recent years, Greece, Chile and Portugal have also fallen victim to deadly wildfires.

FREAK WEATHER

Freak weather is extreme, unexpected weather. There are many different types of freak weather events. Most are sudden, strange and scary. However, the freak weather events that have the greatest impact on people are flash floods (see pages 22–23), ice storms (see pages 24–25), dust storms (see pages 26–27) and heatwaves and drought (see pages 20–21). Here are a few case studies of some of the most devastating freak weather events in history.

HEATWAVE AND DROUGHT CASE STUDY

In 2010, a northern hemisphere heatwave raised temperatures in Russia to a record 44°C. The heatwave sparked the country's worst drought in over 130 years. This led to widespread crop failure across 9 million hectares of farmland. Around 56,000 people died in the heatwave and 55 more during the many wildfires that followed it.

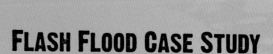

FLASH FLOOD CASE STUDY

In 1979, the deadliest flash flood in history struck the town of Morbi, in Gujarat, India. The flood occurred when unexpected heavy rainfall caused the local Machchhu dam to burst. The dam then sent waves of dust between 3 and 9 m high cascading over Morbi below. Within 20 minutes the town had been flooded and up to 25,000 people killed. The flash flood also destroyed local farmland and led to significant crop damage.

DUST STORM CASE STUDY

America's 'Dust Bowl' was the location of history's most famous dust storm. The 1930s storm struck the US states of Colorado, Kansas, Texas and Oklahoma after grassland was ploughed to grow wheat. This led to over-cultivation of the soil and the development of thin topsoil which was no longer held in place by grassland.

After a drought lasting several years, this top soil was swept away in 'black blizzards' that blocked out the Sun and destroyed local farmlands. Thousands of families were forced to leave the region to start new lives elsewhere.

ICE STORM CASE STUDY

In January 1998, one of the most devastating ice storms on record struck the north-eastern United States and south-eastern Canada.

The ice from the storm reached up to 7.6 cm thick in some areas and caused widespread power cuts. Millions of people were left without power, some for several months. The storm caused 25 deaths from hypothermia and 10 more death from ice-related accidents. The total damage to both countries was estimated to be US$5 billion.

HEATWAVES AND DROUGHT

Heatwaves are periods of excessively high temperatures, which often pose a severe threat to human life. A drought often follows a heatwave when there is less than substantial rainfall. Together, heatwaves and drought cause more deaths than any other natural disaster on Earth. Both are becoming more frequent and extreme as a result of climate change.

HEATWAVES

A heatwave is an extended period where a country's temperatures are far hotter than normal. Usually occurring during the summer, a heatwave can last for several weeks and cause health issues and death. Heat exhaustion, dehydration and heatstroke are commonly suffered, which can be fatal in the young, old and sick.

HEATWAVE FAST FACTS

• Heatwaves are caused by high pressure systems. These systems are caused by descending cool air, which leads to high pressure at the Earth's surface.

• Many countries define a heatwave as 'five or more days with a temperature of 5°C higher than the average for that time of year'.

• Scientists say global warming brought about by climate change will lead to longer and more severe heatwaves in the future.

DROUGHT

A drought is an unusually long dry period with no rain. This can lead to severe shortages of drinking water and damage to crops. As such, a severe drought can be a catastrophe for rural communities. It can lead to crop failure, famine and forced migration away from the drought-stricken areas.

DROUGHT FAST FACTS

- Drought is caused by more water evaporating from the ground than falling in rain.

- Drought can be permanent, seasonal, or take place as part of a freak weather event, such as a heatwave.

- More severe droughts caused by climate change are predicted to have a devastating effect on agriculture in the future.

- While predicting a drought is difficult, one of the easiest steps to take to help prevent the impacts of a drought is to conserve water Then more water will be available when a drought happens.

HEATWAVE-DROUGHT CYCLE

Because there is little rain during a heatwave it often leads to a drought. A drought, in turn, then leads to more heat. This is because there is no water left for the Sun to evaporate. Instead, the Sun heats the land and air. This leads to more heat and a longer drought.

EVAPORATION DECREASES

GROUND DRIES

LESS CHANCE OF RAIN

BREEDS HEAT

FLASH FLOODS

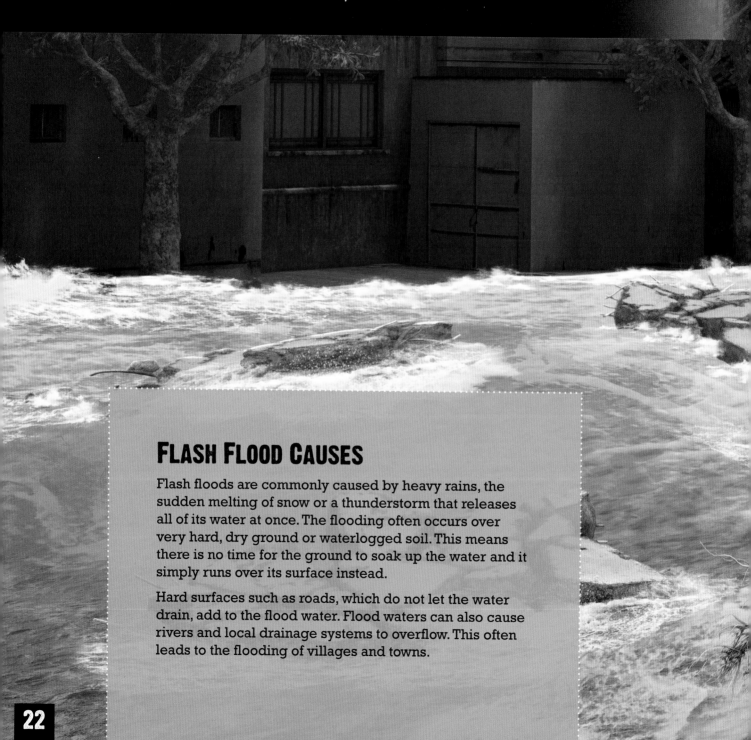

Flash floods are fast, furious weather-related killers that strike without warning. A flash flood can turn a road into a river, wash away people and vehicles, and swamp whole towns with water. Because they are sudden and unpredictable, flash floods often cause many fatalities.

FLASH FLOOD CAUSES

Flash floods are commonly caused by heavy rains, the sudden melting of snow or a thunderstorm that releases all of its water at once. The flooding often occurs over very hard, dry ground or waterlogged soil. This means there is no time for the ground to soak up the water and it simply runs over its surface instead.

Hard surfaces such as roads, which do not let the water drain, add to the flood water. Flood waters can also cause rivers and local drainage systems to overflow. This often leads to the flooding of villages and towns.

FASTER DISASTER FACTS

- Flash floods usually occur over a three- to six-hour period.

- More than half of flash flood fatalities are from people being swept away in their vehicles while trying to escape.

- In urban areas, underground car parks, basements and underpasses can all become death traps during a flash flood.

- When it comes to preventing floods, we cannot stop rain from falling. But we can do something to lessen its impact, such as building retaining walls to stop rivers from bursting, making sure drainage systems are included in town planning, and planting trees and shrubs to reduce the power of moving water and to protect land from erosion.

FLASH FLOOD VALLEY

A flash flood commonly strikes communities living in a river valley. The flood occurs when heavy rain falls quickly onto waterlogged hills above the valley. Because the water cannot soak into the ground, it runs down into the river. The river's water level then rises quickly and bursts its banks, flooding the valley floor.

ICE STORMS

An ice storm is caused by freezing rain that turns into ice when it makes contact with the ground. This can cause objects on the ground to become covered with a layer of smooth ice 20 cm thick. The weight of this ice can then break tree branches and telephone lines and cause major disruption.

ICE STORM IMPACT

Ice storms often occur with little or no warning, but can leave whole cities without electricity by bringing down power lines. When there is no electricity supply for several weeks, the risk of hypothermia increases. Other fatalities can be caused by carbon monoxide poisoning when people without electricity use charcoal, kerosene and propane heaters and barbecues to heat their homes.

- A layer of ice just 3.8 c thick can bring down power lines and make roads too slippery to drive on.

- If partially melted ice from an ice storm then refreezes, treacherous sheets of black ice are formed.

- A 2009 ice storm in the United States caused a 5.1-cm layer of ice that resulted in 55 deaths in Arkansas and Kentucky and left 2 million people were without power.

- The thickest ice from an ice storm was 20 cm, recorded in Idaho, USA, in 1961.

ICE FORMING

An ice storm is caused by rain falling from a layer of air that is above freezing. It then falls into a layer of air that is below freezing. This causes the water droplets to become supercooled and freeze when they hit a solid object, such as a power line or car.

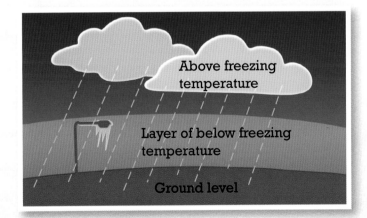

Above freezing temperature

Layer of below freezing temperature

Ground level

DUST STORMS

Dust storms occur when strong winds blow dirt, sand and top soil from one place to another. The storms typically happen in dry, arid regions such as North Africa, the Arabian Peninsula and Central Asia. Airborne particles from dust storms are extremely hazardous to human health and have a devastating effect on agriculture.

DUST STORM FORMING

Large dust storms are often triggered by the powerful winds of a thunderstorm or hurricane. These winds can bounce dust particles along the ground and lift them up to 6,100 m in the air.

Sometimes, a 1.6-km-thick wall of dust is formed and rushes forwards at speeds of 160 kph. This can cause aircraft collisions, road accidents and leave whole houses buried in dust. If breathed in, the dust particles can lead to short- and long-term health problems in people, particularly with their lungs and eyes.

FASTER DISASTER FACTS

- Tiny dust particles are toxic to humans and can cause breathing problems such as asthma, heart stress and eye infections. The dust can also sometimes contain bacteria and disease-carrying spores.

- Every year around 1.5 gigatonnes (1.5 billion tonnes) of dust and sand are carried into Earth's atmosphere.

- A 2009 Australian dust storm ripped 5 million tonnes of topsoil from farmland and deposited it at 75,000 tonnes per hour over the city of Sydney.

- Dust storms also occur on other planets, such as Mars.

DUST PARTICLE MOVEMENT

In a dust storm, the largest particles are moved forwards in a rolling creep motion. Smaller particles between 70 and 500 micrometres hop across the ground in a movement called saltation. Particles smaller than 70 micrometres are lifted high into the atmosphere by the wind in a movement called suspension.

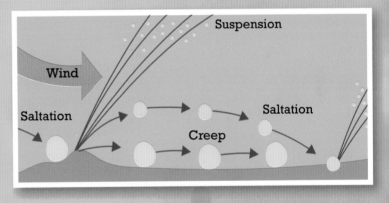

Fish Rain and Orange Snow

Freak weather is normally unusual and unpredictable, but sometimes it can also be frankly bizarre. The strangest freak weather has included orange snow, fish rain and giant hailstones. Some of the most extreme examples of freak weather are explained below.

Raining Fish

As odd as its sounds, a rainfall containing fish is not uncommon. This happens when small tornadoes travel over water, pick up objects such as fish, and drop them elsewhere.

In 2010, hundreds of spangled perch fish fell on the Australian outback town of Lajamanu. The fish were alive when they hit the ground and some residents tried to save them in buckets of water. Rainfalls of toads, tomatoes and coal have also been recorded.

Orange Snow

In 2018, millions of people in eastern Europe were shocked to see orange snow falling from the sky. The snow made the mountains of Ukraine, Russia, Bulgaria and Romania look more like the surface of Mars than a winter landscape. The orange snow was caused by sand from the Sahara Desert mixing with snow and rain. This sand is often lifted into the atmosphere during dust storms and deposited elsewhere (see pages 26-27).

Giant Hailstones

In 1986, giant hailstones weighing up to 1 kg caused 92 deaths in Gopalganj, Bangladesh. The severe hailstorm also injured thousands, destroyed crops and caused damage to homes and buildings. The Gopalganj hailstones were the heaviest on record, but in 2017, hailstones the size of golf balls also hit Turkey and Spain. Such giant hailstones form in tornadoes, where the speed of the wind pushes the ice particles together and freezes raindrops on top. The longer a hailstone spends in a tornado, the larger it gets.

Freak Weather Snap Shots from History

- In 1684, a freak cold snap caused London's River Thames to freeze solid for two months.

- In 2001, a red 'blood' rain fell on parts of India. The colour was caused by airborne spores from an algae. Yellow, green and black rain were also reported.

- In 2009, two Italian archaeologists claimed to have found the skeletons of a vast Persian army, swallowed up by a sandstorm in 524 BCE.

GLOSSARY, BOOKS AND HELPFUL WEBSITES

GLOSSARY

agriculture
The practice of farming, including growing crops and raising animals

arid
Too dry or barren to grow vegetation

arson
The criminal act of setting something on fire on purpose

atmosphere
The blanket of gases around Earth

bush
An area of land covered with bushes and trees that has never been used for growing crops and where there are very few people

carbon monoxide
A colourless, odourless gas that is toxic to humans

class action lawsuit
A lawsuit taken against a company by one person representing a group

climate change
A change in global climate patterns caused by the burning of fossil fuels

dehydration
A harmful loss of water in the human body

displace
Force someone to leave their home because of a natural disaster

drought
A long period when there is little or no rain

ecosystem
A wildlife community that includes plants and animals and their environment

elite
A select group that is considered better in terms of ability or qualities to the rest of a group

erosion
When wind or water gradually wears away at soil, rock or land

grassland
A large area of land covered with grass

heat exhaustion
Tiredness and eventual collapse brought about by exposure to heat

heatstroke
Failure of the body to cool itself down leading to fever and unconsciousness

heatwave
A period of time such as a few weeks when the weather is much hotter than usual

hectare
A unit of measurement of an area of land (10,000 m^2)

hypothermia
Dangerously low body temperature often brought about by exposure to cold

northern hemisphere
The half of the Earth that is above the equator running around its centre

nutrient
Any substance that plants or animals need in order to live and grow

railway sleeper
A long, block of wood that railway tracks lie over

retardant
A substance that prevents the spread of something, such as fire

supercooled
Supercooled liquids have been made colder than the temperature at which they would normally freeze, without being frozen

waterlogged
Full of water and almost covered by a layer of it

BOOKS

Wildfires (Nature Unleashed) by Louise and Richard Spilsbury (Franklin Watts, 2017)

Wildfires (Planet in Peril) by Cath Senker (Wayland, 2014)

Our Planet in Peril by Paul Mason (Wayland, 2018)

Weather (Fact Cat: Science) by Izzi Howell (Wayland, 2018)

HELPFUL WEBSITES

These websites for kids are all about wildfires and extreme forms of weather:

https://easyscienceforkids.com/all-about-wildfires

https://www.ready.gov/kids/know-the-facts/wildfires

http://www.weatherwizkids.com

https://www.metoffice.gov.uk/learning/weather-for-kids

INDEX